Just Like My Dad

By Jayde Frail
Illustrated by Jason Lee

Library For All Ltd.

LIBRARY FOR ALL

DIGITAL EDUCATION · FOR THE WORLD

Library For All is an Australian not for profit organisation with a mission to make knowledge accessible to all via an innovative digital library solution. Visit us at libraryforall.org

Just Like My Dad

First published 2023

Published by Library For All Ltd
Email: info@libraryforall.org
URL: libraryforall.org

Our Yarning logo design by Jason Lee, Bidjipidji Art

Original illustrations by Jason Lee and Michael Magpantay

Just Like My Dad
Frail, Jayde
ISBN: 978-1-922991-99-7
SKU01396

Just Like My Dad

2

My name is Nicholas and this is my dad. He is my best friend.

When I grow up, I want
to be just like him.

My dad builds rock walls, paves paths and makes beautiful gardens.

I always help my dad
when he is working on
weekends.

I dig the ground for plants and water the area to make it soft.

I push the wheelbarrow and clear leaves and branches.

I watch my dad use all the noisy machines to help him work.

My dad says one day, when I'm old enough, I can use the machines too.

I just can't wait!

I want to be a landscaper.

Just like my dad.

You can use these questions to talk about this book with your family, friends and teachers.

What did you learn from this book?

Describe this book in one word. Funny? Scary? Colourful? Interesting?

How did this book make you feel when you finished reading it?

What was your favourite part of this book?

About the contributors

Jayde was born in Coota Mundra in New South Wales and now lives in Canberra. She is from the Nyempa/Gamilaroi Nations in Brewarrina. Jayde likes to tell stories and, as a child, her favourite book was *Fox in Sox* by Dr Seuss.

Jason Lee is a Larrakia man, born and living in Darwin. He loves drawing and being with his family. His favourite story is *The Very Hungry Caterpillar*.

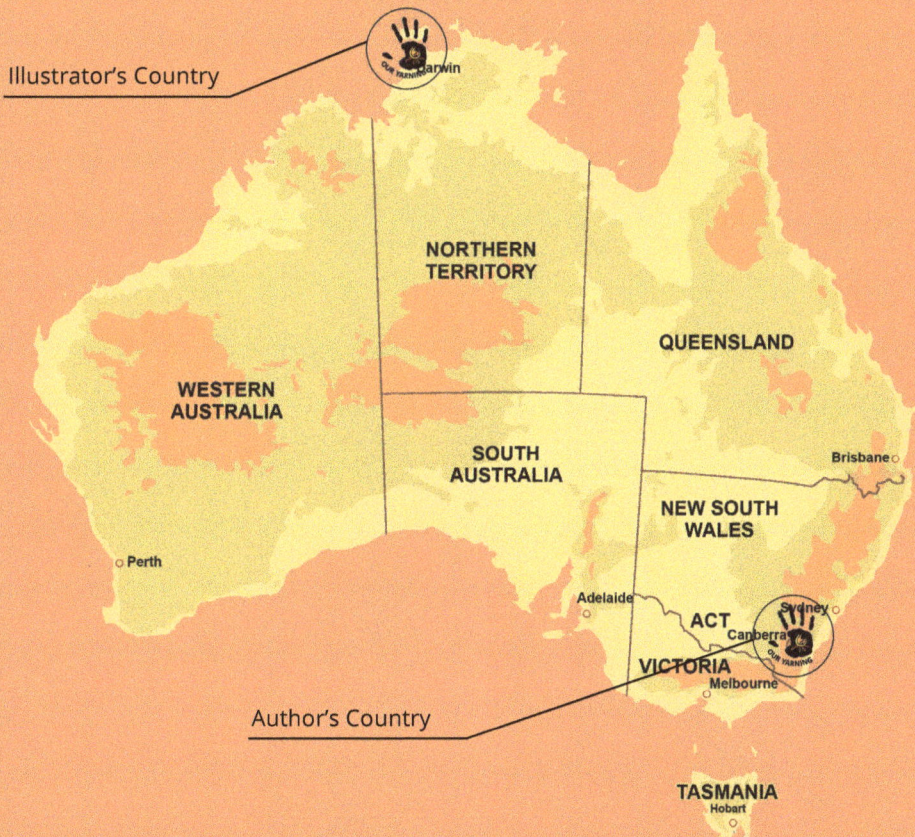

Illustrator's Country

Darwin

NORTHERN
TERRITORY

QUEENSLAND

WESTERN
AUSTRALIA

SOUTH
AUSTRALIA

Brisbane

NEW SOUTH
WALES

Perth

Adelaide

ACT
Canberra

Sydney

VICTORIA
Melbourne

Author's Country

TASMANIA
Hobart

Our Yarning

Want to discover more books from this collection? Our Yarning is a collection of books written by Aboriginal and Torres Strait Islander peoples across Australia.

We know that children learn better, and enjoy reading more, when they see themselves in the stories, characters and illustrations of the books they read.

To download the app, visit the Google Play Store on any Android device and search 'Our Yarning'.

www.ingramcontent.com/pod-product-compliance
Lightning Source LLC
Chambersburg PA
CBHW042347040426
42448CB00019B/3440